Long Exposure
At Cordoba

Katherine Crocker

Indigo Dreams Publishing

First Edition: Long Exposure at Cordoba
First published in Great Britain in 2012 by:
Indigo Dreams Publishing
132 Hinckley Road
Stoney Stanton
Leicestershire
LE9 4LN

www.indigodreams.co.uk

ISBN 978-1-907401-66-4

British Library Cataloguing in Publication Data. A CIP record for this book can be obtained from the British Library.

Designed and typeset in Palatino Linotype by Indigo Dreams.

Cover design and illustrations by Joseph Crocker.

Printed and bound in Great Britain by The Russell Press Ltd. www.russellpress.com on FSC paper and board sourced from sustainable forests.

Acknowledgements

Acknowledgements are due to the editors of the following publications in which some of these poems first appeared: Acumen, Ambit, Interpreter's House, Iota, Orbis, Other Poetry, Reach Poetry, Smiths Knoll and The Rialto.

In 2006 and 2007 two of these poems were commended in the Blinking Eye competition and appeared in the anthologies, *Night Balancing* and *Blood Line*, respectively. Also in 2007 the poem, *Lovers, Belarus*, was runner up in the Writers Inc, writer-of-the-year competition and published in the anthology, *Dropped Notes*. In 2009 two poems, *Long Exposure at Cordoba* and *Istanbul, 1995*, appeared in the Templar Poetry Pamphlet Prize anthology, *Stripe*.

Thanks are due to Carole Bromley, Antony Dunn and Nick Rennison who have given much support during the writing of this book. Finally, thanks to all the friends at Guppy's Tuesday writing group.

CONTENTS

Long Exposure
At Cordoba

"Stories can save us if we use our imagination." Scheherazade

Long Exposure at Cordoba

You took a photo in the dusk,
midday pink at the mosque,
repeated shadows and arches
patterned like fugues.

You focussed the camera,
light reading at the centre,
perfect image to remember
the church within.

But when you get the print
the stone is blurred,
my ghost walks towards you
in orange blossom scent.

Heather

A handful of twigs, tied with white string,
spikes of green, tasting of moors.
Each lilac flower like a tiny stuffed purse,
a purple bead's weight.

A posy of smoke and damp dirt
from his January garden – *good luck* –
he said, for the child, eight hours old,
her eyes tight shut.

And I salted the woody stems,
pressed them in the pages of Africa,
preserved the treasure of love meant,
though he never said that.

Shadow Man

At bedtime we play shadow puppets
when the landing light's on
and the curtains shut out the moon.

But when the landing light is off,
our game is over. My brother still sees
the shadow man's face and long fingers.

He climbs into my bed. *Tell me a story*
of the brave boy, the one-eyed giant,
twelve princesses. We sleep in the dark.

Two hundred miles and fifty years
are no distance for the shadow man.
Now we dream with the night light on.

Daphne

The tree splits, reaches to another sun,
pink arms flesh green, tiny buds
open from her finger tips. Her spine
twists, shrinks in green stems, thuds
down and within her ribs the wood
laces lungs, heart, liver. Trapped
by Apollo's speed, sap pales her blood,
seeps through his hands wrapped
round her waist. He stops her mouth,
his kisses rip on splinters. In curls of cork
he whispers love; too late his breath
deadens in shells, once ears, now bark.
The last he sees of her, one tear of amber
and it's not pity for him, but anger.

About Time

The clock strikes ten as she walks into the hall.
A perfume of rose petals disguises the stench
of dancers' sweat and tallow candle grease.
Her dress, sewn by magicians, has spangles
of coloured glass and beneath silk underskirts
she's hidden her favourite kitchen knife.

Wine in silver punch bowls, sweetmeats
and pastries heaped on malachite tables
and ivory counters. The guests drink and eat
beyond reason as she calculates her chance,
she dances with counts, dukes and princes.
This is the last time she'll wear glass slippers.

Eleven o' clock, the musicians still play.
The violinist watches her – she returns his gaze,
steps behind stone pillars to consider: maybe
in time she could elope with him, live in attic rooms
forever. She catches his eye, walks to the garden
through yew trees in jasmine-scented breezes.

It's after midnight when she runs home,
slips through the back door. No candle smuts
or blood on her old clothes. She mends the fire,
pours a bowl of soup and waits for her father
to return with terrible news: his wife and
step-daughters have been brutally murdered.

She listens to the story about the violinist
caught red-handed, moon-mad from the deed
at the scene of the crime but insisted he'd not
done it. He said he'd a witness but no-one
came forward. She gave her father some soup,
cut the bread with her favourite kitchen knife.

The Road

When they left,
the road didn't seem so long.
And while they waited
at the border,
they often talked
of their journey home.

The time came
for the women to walk back.
Bags lost or left at camps,
their children carried sacks
of seeds to plant
in their fields at home.

And the road
churned in mud,
crumbled under foot.
Between carts abandoned
by the wayside,
they trudged home.

In orchard trees
they found their sons,
flightless kites blowing
in the wind. Black shapes
stretched in branches,
their husbands' faces
looked down on them,
on the road home.

Circus

Sometimes I am the clown,
play the slap-stick fool,
fall over my shoes
just to hear you laugh.

Then I walk on stilts,
ride the circus cycle,
tumble through hoops
to see you gasp

as my outsized slippers
trip on high wires, miss
the acrobat's clasp, to hold
you in a cloud of rosin.

I pretend I'm flying
but really I'm falling
when my spot-lit shadow
cartwheels to your side.

Smell the torches
spinning around you.
I'm eating fire, my lips burn,
kiss you on the mouth.

Snake, Choeung Ek

Something slithers in the mud
slips through the rainy season,
through long grass, something
thin, muscular, looking for food.

We walk in a field of trees,
stained with blood, on marquetry
of earth and bones, silent until
something slithers in the grass.

Thirty years ago, her mother hid
a snake in her skirt, her teeth
bit off the head, her lips
caked in mud. But they ate meat,

something they'd not done, she said,
not since her father had left
in the rainy season and his clothes
returned, folded dry, caked in mud.

Now she gasps at the snake's
green flash, broken in the grass,
tells me her mother lied when they asked
how old she was. She was eight.

So we walk on bones broken
by machetes, polished by shoes.
My shoes on folded rags, blindfolds,
blue, green, stained with blood.

My feet on teeth, broken from skulls,
washed by rain from the path
and among wet grass something
slithers and my companion laughs.

She saw her mother's eyes fixed
on the snake, shook rice from the basket,
folded the trap in a ripple of water.
They did not speak. No-one did.

The snake was harmless, looking for food.
Never enough. We walk in wet grass
looking at blood and nine thousand
skulls racked in a white pagoda.

She says the magic tree played music,
no-one heard bones breaking.
They turned a blind eye, green and blue,
blindfolds caked in mud.

Now the snake brought a flood
of memory, some things she'd not thought
for years, about her sisters looking for food,
fruit and leaves in winter woods.

And her brother coming home
when it was over. Though he never spoke
of what he'd done, just walked in the sun,
carved toys for children and tourist trinkets.

See the snake slither, slip
through wet grass, on broken bones,
down into the pits of headless graves.
We walk on long paths, shoes caked in mud.

Lovers, Belarus

It was an ordinary picnic,
red printed cloth,
wine flask and bread.

They sat where two rivers
met, flowed as one,
felt the breeze on their face.

On the opposite bank
painted houses, dirt track
to the orthodox church.

Before he caught his breath
her red dress blew
about her legs, lifted

her feet off the ground.
In one hand he held
the bird, in the other

her hand as she glided
up, over the town.
And if he wanted to keep her

swimming in air,
he had to hold his grip,
float with her.

Together over Vitebsk,
poultry yards, cow barns,
meadows, she held out her arm.

The fiddler playing a jig,
soldier with bread, stopped,
watched them fly

over raggy topped fences,
red and green houses.
They didn't speak of the child

but everyone could see
he held on, kept her close
in the clouds over the town.

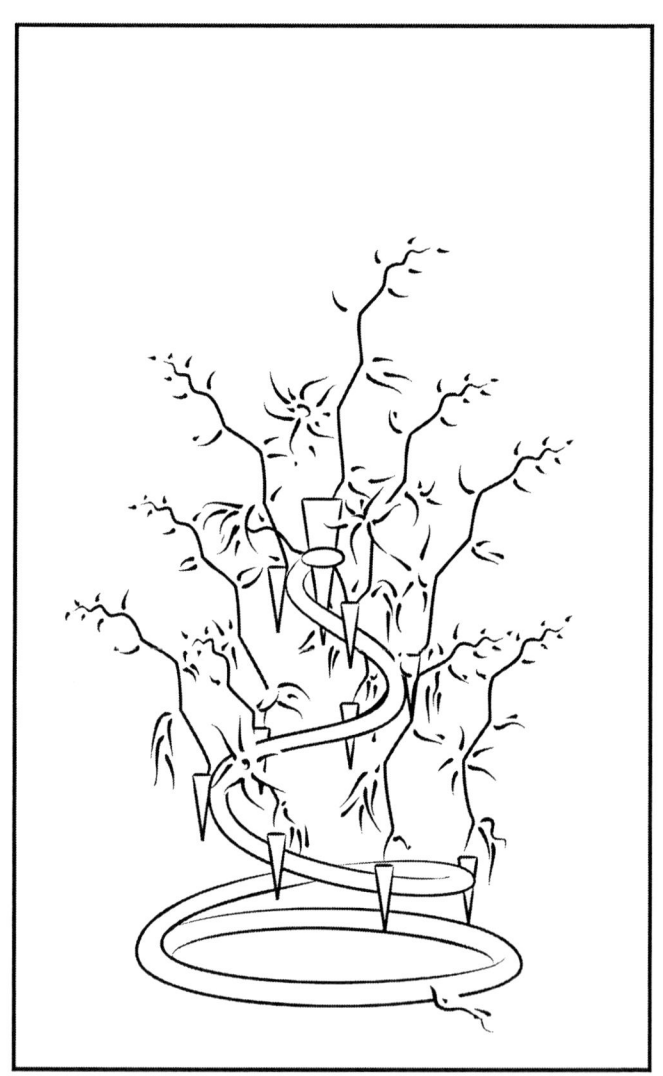

Lighthouse

It was in August 1959
when I went to the house on the headland
to be my grandmother's eyes.

Each morning we had breakfast on the cliff top,
then counted a hundred and fifty two steps
down to the rock pools.

We swam among gulls
waiting for fishermen to return,
seaweed salt fastened in our throats.

In the afternoons, sleeping on warm white pebbles,
she wept when I picked montbretia
for the spiral silver vase.

At night, the lighthouse lulled us to sleep.
I reckoned the seconds on the chrome alarm clock,
counted the measure of dark and blink of light.

Years later she told me *You saved my life.*
Pop died in the Spring. I was on the edge …
but you picked montbretia for the spiral silver vase.

Flying at Heimaey

Over the cliff of volcanic rock, kelp-brown,
he leans, where the harbour Atlantic spray
soaks the young puffins as they struggle to fly.
He stands in basalt ash, still hot, remains
of folded rock heaved into islanders' homes –
twenty years of Arctic rain has not cooled it.
I tell him that once these rocks made stars,
families boarded boats, sailed for three days,
while fishermen hosed lava at the mouth
of the harbour. But what does he discover?
Not that volcanoes fume on the ocean floor
but there's a tiny shudder in the puffin's heart
held in his ten-year old hands as he throws the bird
to the wind and new wings fly for the first time.

Wounded

Early summer he came without invitation.
She had no chance to turn him away before
he slumped into her kitchen, wounded,
blood-soaked fur, matted black, evidence
of the wire trap.

As he slept she prepared a poultice
of elm and flaxseed for his broken paw,
hanging limp and useless, the tendon
exposed through torn flesh. She wrapped it
in comfrey and muslin.

All season she tended his wound until
the scar held firm. She hid her gun, smiled
to see him run. Her neighbours laced loops
of razor wire around their orchard gates,
closed their windows.

She left her windows open, could hear
his kind calling him home, knew he listened
but still he stayed. She took him to her bed,
kept the gun under her pillow, fed him
wine and candy.

There was no breeze, the blankets thrown
aside, his mended paw on her breast, her face
close to his. They slept. Her neighbours crept
into the house, cut his throat, they said they did it
to protect her.

Lilacs

She carries lilacs into her house
like the baby she's never had,
cradled in her arms,
sheltered from the wind.

All morning she's cut nettles,
twining briars, bindweed threads
to untangle the purple flowers
falling over the hedge.

Now the cherished blossoms
are in jars, kissing the air
to wake her. Armfuls of blue
perfume every room.

Istanbul, 1995

On the bend in the road
she walked straight
into the headlights of a car.
Her brains spilt at my feet.

The shopkeeper rushed out
put old newspapers over her face
washed my shoes
returned to her customers.

The police directed the traffic
around the heap of old news.
My taxi arrived.
I had dinner at the hotel.

The Square

They came to the square,
shopkeeper, teacher and butcher's errand boy,
to listen to the speeches,
brought thermos flasks, primus stoves,
stayed all day.   At night they left,
swept the square.

Next day they came
to hear the judge's verdict, no jury called,
the government of the people
found everyone guilty.
Shopkeeper, teacher and butcher's errand boy
slept in the square.

Next day the soldiers came,
shot without hesitation, shopkeeper, teacher,
and the butcher's errand boy
who left home for a loaf of bread.
The soldiers brought water
to clean the square.

Kale Field

Beneath purple veins and shaded green,
amongst trampled stalks we made our den.
Kale so tall we were hidden all afternoon,
nestled in willow herb we'd hauled
from the hedge. For years the field
had been tansy and yarrow but Dad built
clay drains, planted new crops,
had seven cows, a deal at the bank.

From our hidey hole we watched his knife,
raised three times as he plunged the steel
through swollen flesh, calves gorged on kale
and gas oozed from silver rings bubbling red
until their reshaped bodies filled with life.
He pushed them to take a step and they left
the field as it was. Kale so tall we were hidden
all afternoon but for the tell-tale open gate.

Landing

Once concrete blocks and barbed wire
scribed this shore and this is where
he took me sailing among the relics of the war,
he showed me how he loved the sea.

The wind blew, we leaned to the north,
sixteen foot of fibre-glass straining.
She's breaking up, pull the centre board.
The boat slammed full weight on the stony floor.

Now the waves suck and spit on clean sand
and there are no boats, but my pulse races.
The same east wind shoves on the heave of sea.
Signs warn of the current's undertow.

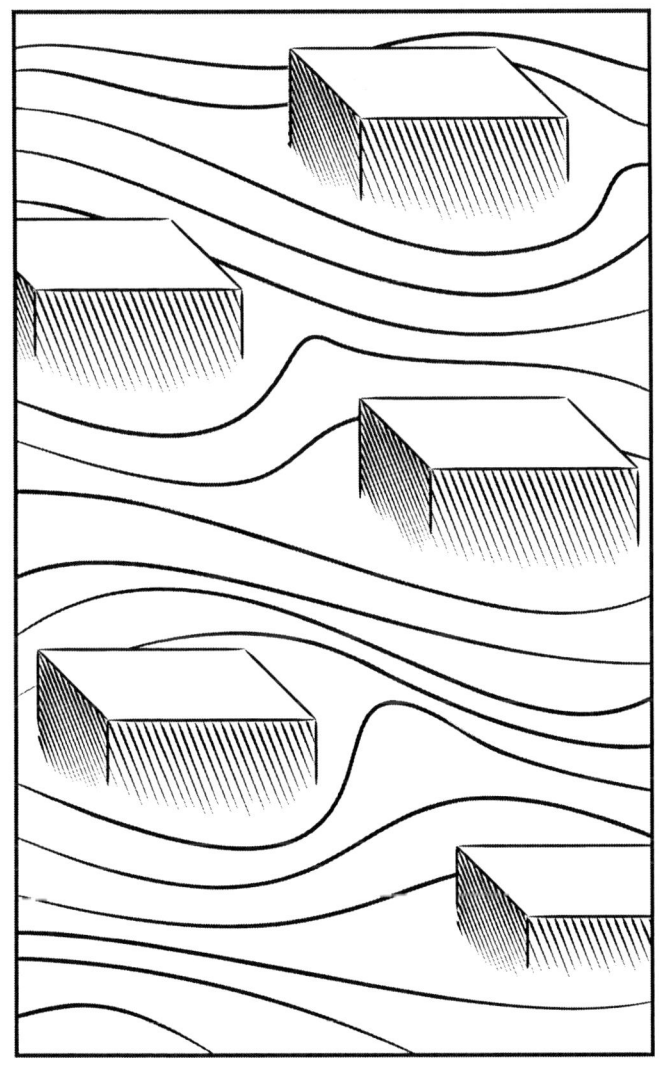

Silt

There's a weight of dirt, each grain
      of earth dragging over and over
            until grits and grey-green mud, life bloods,
swirl and spawn in the heave of water

      shifting curls of soil slicks, whirlpools
            spinning a thread of land, rock spits,
sand-made islands and paths further
      along where the dam holds back

            this fertile-flow, a host of minerals.
So the shape of the river bed is not fixed,
      but retraces and retreats across
            invisible borders; connects and dis-

connects places.   And when silt feeds
      a new-grown crop, to bless
            this river, then Yuan prays it will never stop
bringing its cargo of goodness

      re-routed through his mountains.
            This new river runs to where grain
is abundant and Yuan can sell
      to the people at the border.

            And the old river is finished,
dried to dust, the sown seeds
      are blown in the wind, wasted in the dry land
            after the dam.

Alchemy

In her kitchen she whisks cream for puddings
brandy chocolate mousse and coconut tarts.
Cupboards hoarding sugar, almonds and sloe gin
the chemistry of cooking – her secret art.

Thin skin like Japanese paper
she smells of butterscotch and Foxes mints.

At night she unlaces her coral bone corset.
I witness the unveiling from under the sheets.
She studies her face and combs her gold hair
in magical mirrors of infinite partitions.

In this place of transformation, I shut my eyes,
hear her teeth sink in the water.
She closes her drawers on the potions and hairnets
Elizabeth Arden and Pond's Night Cream.

She turns off the light and climbs into bed.
There we are, Grandma and me.

I'm a magician

Your calloused toes first
to disappear,
walk barefoot
in Merzouga dunes.
I never liked your feet.

Your strong legs next,
mountain strides
climb Todra Gorge.
Every muscle melts
in the midday heat.

Your folded arms,
soft hairs and sunburn,
right over left, patiently
wait to fall away
at Meknes palace.

Your square hands,
farmer and scholar
combine your grip,
your hold slips,
easy and painless.

Your voice is almost
last to go.   You say
we're the same, but
Marrakesh is airless.
I have no answer.

Your black eyes last,
your final look as though
I should know.
I close the box,
my final gesture.

And the trick is
not that you've vanished,
piece by piece,
but when I'm curious
I can lift the lid.

Somewhere

There's a camel sleeping
with one eye open,
a scorpion hiding
under a stone.

There's a hawk flying
over the dune.
It's as it should be
but you're not here.

You said you'd be back
when stars were shooting.
I thought it a good sign
of new beginnings.

But your letter says nothing
of where you are,
when you're returning.
Only one explanation:

the stars are fading,
not like corn shoots
in soft rain and earth –
for these I've been waiting.

All you say is –
the shooting stars
are not shooting,
they are dying.

Ghosts

She lies still waiting for sleep.
The bed, an island of dim light,
moon-cast shadows of date palms
on adobe walls. But her love
makes no shadow. Outside,
sand blows at the door, lizards hide
under stones. She half expects
his voice in the dark, whisper
her name. She wants to tell him
about the mistletoe that grows
by the road in the Atlas Mountains,
green stem and berries she's picked
for him. But his love is sand
re-shaping dunes every night.

She feels his breath in her ear,
turns to listen. Their tongues,
nothing to say, touch. Her love
is the ocean tide, waves heaped
on the shore. She waits for sunset,
soft murmurs when boys fish for squid
at low ebb, she slips into rock pools
where he's waited all this time
in the shallows. He kisses
her forehead, she falls asleep.

Trekking

His face barely visible behind white and red check,
the boy hissed through his teeth, my camel's arse
reared up. I'm pushed forward in the saddle
then the front legs unfold, we lollop onward.
Long shadows, the sun behind us, Wadi Rum
in front. Seven pillars of pink sandstone.
The boy rattled his throat, we began to trot
toward the Bedouin tent sheltered under the cliff
and there we told stories on the way to Aqabar.
By the campfire under the desert's shooting stars,
a Roc could have arched his wings over that place
and we wouldn't have noticed the white feather quills
fall. On the radio we heard the map-maker
was drawing another line, another boundary.

Eurydice's story

He played like no-one I'd heard before.
His lyre, his voice, lulled me in a trance
until I danced through fields and forest
to our wedding feast. The water nymphs
guessed it would not last, happiness
like this, even for greater gods is rare.
So when the bee keeper came on that day,
I had no chance, though I ran like a hare.
Orpheus sang. The snake bit.

All his songs, laments, couldn't wake me,
slumped on the stream's moss bank,
my last breath caught in his lyre's strings
and his soft kiss on my cheek, still warm.
My dying breath would not rest, played
on the strings a song of such loss,
the gods could not forget our sadness.
They blessed us, promised Orpheus
would rescue me from oblivion.

So he played, Cerebus slept. The Styx
filled with tears, even Erinyes wept.
Hades listened, promised I could follow
Orpheus when he left. He would play,
back to earth, not look back. Simple,
you would have thought. And so did I
as we walked long stony paths to the sun,
smelled lilacs, felt the forest's gasp.
Then he turned around. Why?

Now I live among the heat and sulphur.
A hell of wishing I was back on earth,
the rain, the snow, sun and songs.
Does anyone remember how I sang,
my last arpeggio spun in silver,
the wonder of why it ended as it did
when all he had to do was play,
not turn around, just one thing –
but he turned and looked for me.

Autumn

Allotment fires smoke
over the path as we walk
home in the silent fading light –
months of misty mornings
and dark nights to come.

But when we talk
it's not of this, but our visit
to Pottsdam in '96
when we ran down
terraced steps, kicked leaves
as high as our heads,
crackling amber and topaz,
jewel-lit in afternoon light,
more precious
than all Fredrick's treasure
in his palace hall of mirrors.

Life lines

Her head is fallen back, her mouth open.
A red thread links to her arm, at her neck
a thin yellow line drips sleep 'til morning.

We wait in this cool room, its green
light and high windows, for the early sun
to greet us. We're wrapped in fleeces.

All night, monitors flash primary colours,
lines and numbers, maps of every moment
she has. I ask the nurse to turn off the bleep

but the lines she keeps and so we watch
graphs and waves, lines on wired screens
and try to rest behind half-closed curtains.

She looks so young. Her skin, translucent
in the ward light. Her fingers, thinner,
like the hands of a musician. I hold them.

I want to paint red lipstick on her mouth,
contours of the laugh I know and on each eye,
a line of kohl, where I last saw tears.

Mud

Cracked rivulets of brown, taste of salt,
river and sea meet at high tide in eddied reeds
and the silt tells the story of the changed land.
He walks on the bank, letter in his pocket, opened
and folded but he wants to forget it, one more day.

Summer almost over, dust in the corn driers,
his son stands in the yard agreeing final prices.
Tomorrow he will tell him, no more secrets,
tell him straight. But the heron is stealing trout
from the still waters of the pond he'd built.

Cold metal on his cheek, sight fixed on the heron,
one or two shots to scare it. Sea mist blurs,
eyelids close, water rushes over the ploughed field.
A wood to the west, the bank broken to the east.
Kitty's yellow hair in the tall wheat.

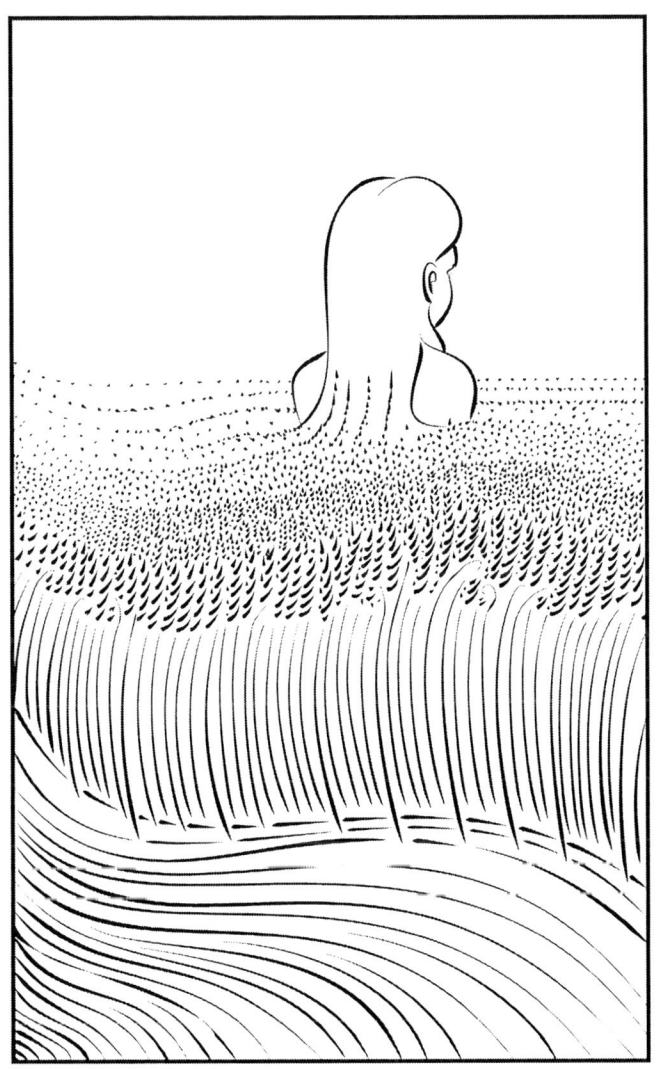

Segou, November 2008
inspired by Amadou Kone's love poems

I watch women wash their clothes,
bathe in suds, gossip about their men
on the banks of the River Niger.

At the jetty, the ferryboy rows, girls clamber
to the shore, balance zinc bowls of smoked fish
and a man carries his bicycle.

It's my last afternoon in Segou when Amadou
arrives, strong arms levering his wheelchair
up the dirt road to the Rablais hotel.

At the market you can buy clay pots,
chilli, shea butter, plastic buckets, soap
and crocodile claws. Amadou sells poems.

I had malaria as a child then polio too,
he says. *I'm training to be an accountant.*
My poems pay for school.

Boys, with their donkeys and carts, load
sorgum and millet. *You can buy anything here,*
he says. I push his chair over ruts.

He takes me to the medicine man where
wishes are sold. Tiny pins and parchment scraps,
sewn and folded, to burn or keep.

Amadou dreams of an office job, a wage.
He pulls his thin legs from the chair, rests his feet
in red street dust. It's sunset.

We read poems to each other under dim
market lamps. Words, not translated, sing out,
music in different tongues.

Today is a great day, Amadou smiles.
Can any day really make such a difference?
I ask, buy a book of poems.

About us the market sellers stop and listen, light
their fires for the night, hold their hands
on hearts, shout *Obama, Obama.*

Bones

Sometimes when I sit,
spine bent forward in this chair,
hunched, waiting for breath,
I drink a cup of tea.
My elbows rest
on green velvet arms,
now a family heirloom,
though so worn, valueless.
The shape of repose,
visible since he left,
hugs at my back –
it's not me.

I hold the mug,
right hand on the handle,
the other circling the rim,
and it's his neat fingers,
nails tendency to flake.
My face warm,
leans over the steam –
I am him.

Bone-tired,
out since dawn.
He's called the cows in,
walked to Clay Field
and back to the farm.
Still got his wellies on.

I am him
I feel him in my bones.

Damage

Bumble bees, someone once told me,
can carry weights of pollen and nectar
for almost two miles back to their cells,
a little more food than they need,
inside wax walls.

Walls, when shells storm, drones buzz,
bubble-wrap homes are no shelter,
melt in heat. White phosphorous mats
smoulder on flour sacks, fire flashes
in grain and dust.

Dust in shelters, children wrapped
in folded blankets, like silk cocoons,
they're safely kept. But after the blast,
parents collect the tiny charred bodies
from their nest.

Nests are craters that once were homes.
At a party once, someone told me,
bumble bees start again, if the Queen's
safe. Survivor workers build another nest
after the damage.

Judith

His fortress love was no comfort to you,
listening
at closed doors, granite walls sighing.

Your love for him was greedy, wheedling
until he weakened
and embraced you, his pocket full of keys.

You thought you'd have the whole of him,
doors opened –
ropes, rapiers, rubies, a robin's nest.

It was hard to stop, addicted and frenzied
with no end,
until you wept – one key left unspun.

Though you smelt the flesh, still couldn't resist.
He turned
kissed your mouth full of blood.

This is the boundary

This is the field where trees were felled,
heaped and loaded on carts, taken
to rot in the orchard, nurtured
in spring for the autumn fruit.

This is the road where windfalls were swept,
heaped and loaded on carts, blown
with maggots, ruined and shovelled
to a mound of blight and mould.

This is the orchard, where apples were picked,
heaped and loaded on carts, taken
to store in turf-roofed sheds, locked
and left for a winter of hunger.

In this broken place, all that's left to teach us,
barbed wire fences, rotten harvest breezes.

Buttons

You can tell a lot from buttons –
they hold us together,
not like zippers or poppers,
but ostentatiously different.

For my Christmas present in '84
you gave me a biscuit tin,
embossed with flowers,
gold scrolls, cobalt rim –
full of buttons.

Some were sewn on cards,
others in families on linen thread
but most were loose and shifting places.
Wooden toggles for sailors' hands
jostled shirt, trousers, farmers' buttons,
sometimes four holes, sometimes two
or jet octagons with just one loop.
For art deco dressmakers' deft stitch
there were coral cameos, lovers' pearls,
silver leaves, painted china squares.
And gold, industrially pressed for soldiers,
uniform buttons long past, and hand-carved,
and fabric-covered, and sea-blue glass.
Yellow and white daisy buttons
for miners' mothers' Sunday best.

And the pleasure
was not one single button
but pushing my hand
through the depth of them.

Winter

Sainte Colombe shunned the court
when the birds fledged in late spring,
played his viola de gamba in the summer house
while the sparrows flew and sang
between branches of the mulberry tree.

His long fingers pressed down on gut frets,
smoothed seven silver-spun strings,
played songs for lovers, unrequited laments,
like ripples on lakes or treacherous seas
calling for sailors to return to the harbour.

The resistance of the low notes resonated
like pebbles in the undertow.
His bow was water, ebbing and flowing
in perfect metre. Double stops and suspensions
dissolved to pianissimo.

Throughout the autumn the courtiers said
he'd return to the palace but he stayed in his garden,
muted under a blanket of snow, he played
new improvisations, wild and distant.
Does it matter that nobody heard him?

When scholars returned the following spring,
the notes he played were weeping streams
of melted snow, ripples of sorrow.
They could only imagine the icy brilliance,
his music before the crack of thaw.

La Peregrina Pearl

Jacopo Trezzo, the King's jeweller, said
a Spanish slave found this pearl a hundred
feet down on the Panama seabed.

With a spear he used to fight off sharks,
he dived, held his breath for three minutes
as he prized the oyster from the ocean rocks.

I want to be that pearl, a treasure collected
from black depths, a fortune paid,
a gift for a lover in her royal wedding bed.

And you shall pay the greatest cost,
ensure I'm never lost and the slave, who risked
his life to find me, will be free at last.

I'm one droplet made of a hundred layers
of microscopic hexagons of aragonite. A tear
fashioned from struggle, nacre's lustre,

to alleviate the pain of a particle of grit
against sensitive skin, a perfect fit.
You, my hero; me, your comfort.

Postscript

Snowdrops hang
shut tight.
They resist
the January light,
keep their secret
one more night.

I count the days
of the coaxing sun,
hold my breath,
pray for the flowers
to open.

Each year's the same,
I cannot begin
without them.

Notes

The poem *Winter* is written about the French seventeenth century composer who until recently has been a mysterious figure. He was primarily noted for his virtuoso compositions on the viola de gamba, although little else was recorded. Recent research suggests something of his background but he never sought fame, or indeed, published his music.

Indigo Dreams Publishing
132, Hinckley Road
Stoney Stanton
Leicestershire
LE9 4LN
www.indigodreams.co.uk